All About My Christmas

by JOAN WALSH ANGLUND

with EMILY ANGLUND-NELLEN

SCHOLASTIC INC.

New York Toronto London Auckland Sydney

ISBN 0-590-41523-9

12 11 10 9 8 7 6 5 4 3 2 1   9/8 0 1 2 3 4/9
Printed in the U.S.A.   36

Design by Tracy Arnold

First Scholastic printing, October 1989

Christmas is coming...
Soon there will be
holly and tinsel
and a star
on each tree.

Christmas is coming...
Soon Santa and sleigh
will visit each home,
leaving gifts
on his way.

Christmas is coming...
the season is near
when hearts are all merry
and filled with
good cheer.

My Christmas

My name is _____.

This will be my _____ Christmas.

We will celebrate this Christmas at

_____ with

_____.

What do I like *best* about Christmas?

_____

_____.

...the many things we DO to get ready for Christmas!

(Color the circle next to the things *you* do!)

○ Selecting tree

○ Mailing cards and packages

○ Decorating tre

○ Shopping

○ Wrapping gifts

○ Writing Christmas car

The Busy Days of Christmas

○ Going to church

○ Giving a Christmas party

○ Decorating house

○ Visiting Santa

○ Going caroling

○ Delivering gifts

My Most "Wished-For" Gift

Draw a picture of the gift you would like most for Christmas this year.

Help Fill Santa's Bag

NORTH POLE

Please help fill Santa's bag with toys and gifts for christmas

DRAW IN THE THINGS SANTA
WILL BRING TO ALL THE BOYS and GIRLS.

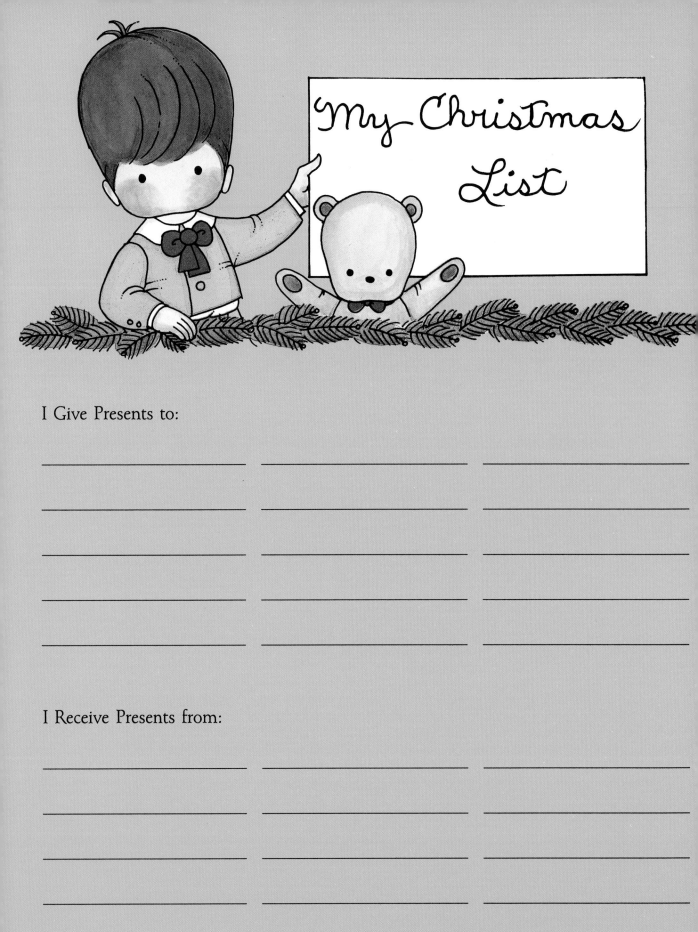

My Christmas List

I Give Presents to:

_____ _____ _____

_____ _____ _____

_____ _____ _____

_____ _____ _____

_____ _____ _____

I Receive Presents from:

_____ _____ _____

_____ _____ _____

_____ _____ _____

_____ _____ _____

Christmas Cards

My family and I sent Christmas cards to:

_____ _____ _____

_____ _____ _____

_____ _____ _____

_____ _____ _____

_____ _____ _____

_____ _____ _____

_____ _____ _____

This Christmas my family and I received_____Christmas cards.

Which card came from farthest away?_____.

Which card arrived first?_____ Date_____

My favorite card was from_____.

My Favorite Christmas Cards

(Paste in the card your family sent this year)

(Paste in the best card your family received)

My Favorite Christmas Cards

December
Days

25

FILL IN YOUR ACTIVITIES ON THE CALENDAR AS YOU COUNT DOWN
TO CHRISTMAS.

The Gifts of Christmas

We buy many of our gifts...but the MOST REMEMBERED gifts at Christmas are the gifts we *made*...all by ourselves!

Color in the circles next to the ways *you* made gifts this year.

○ Woodwork

○ Cutting and Pastin

○ Claywork

○ Painting or Draw

○ Cooking and Baking

Draw a picture of a gift you made.

List other ways to make gifts:

○ Sewing and Knitting

_____

_____

_____

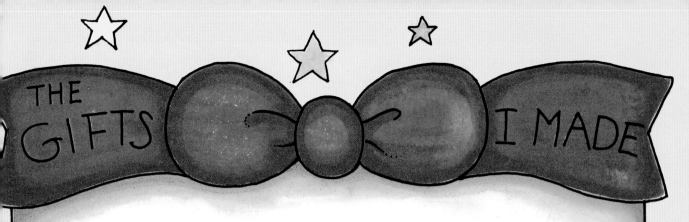

THE GIFTS I MADE

Christmas is for giving, and of all the gifts at Christmas the *very best* gift is the gift of ourselves — of our caring, our helpfulness, and the love we show to one another...because that gift lasts all year through!

_____ for _____

_____ for _____

_____ for _____

_____ for _____

_____ for _____

_____ for _____

_____ for _____

_____ for _____

(List the gift)   (List the person who received it)

O Christmas Tree

Our Christmas tree is Beautiful
Our Christmas tree is Special

This year...

Who chose the tree? _____

Where did we find it? _____

We put our tree up on _____

Who helped decorate the tree? _____

_____

This year our tree was:

Skinny ☐   Short ☐   Fat ☐   Tall ☐

Medium ☐   Small ☐   Just Right ☐

Real ☐   Artificial ☐

The Best Ever ☐

The First Christmas Tree

It was a cold winter night in Germany in 1605. Martin Luther was walking through a dark forest when he saw a tree lighted by stars. He took home a small fir tree and lit it with candles, so he could share with his family the beauty he had seen.

This is the legend of the first Christmas tree.

Decorate the Tree...

Draw your favorite ornament on the tree.

Where did it come from?_____

_____

The Songs of Christmas

Circle the drawing next to the songs you can sing.

 Christmas Tree   Frosty the Snowman

 Silent Night   Jingle Bells

 Deck the Halls   Joy to the World

 We Three Kings   White Christmas

 Away In a Manger   Oh, Little Town of Bethlehem

 O Come All Ye Faithful   Rudolph the Red-Nosed Reindeer

Name other Christmas songs you sing.

_____

_____

_____

What is your favorite Christmas song?

_____

The First Christmas

And the Angel said unto Mary and Joseph,
"Fear not! For Behold!
I bring you good tidings of great joy!"
(St. Luke 2:10)

"We have seen His star," said the Wise Men,
"and are come to worship Him."
(St. Matthew 2:2)

They saw the Young Child with Mary His mother
and fell down and worshipped Him
And when they had opened their treasures
they presented Him with gifts:
Gold, Frankincense, and Myrrh.
(St. Matthew 2:11)

For unto us a Child is born
...and His name shall be called
the Prince of Peace.
(Isiah 9:6)

Glory to God in the Highest
...and on Earth, Peace
and Goodwill toward men!
(St. Luke 2:14)

Draw in a picture of the Star of Bethlehem, which led the Wise Men to the manger.

The Tastes of Christmas

This was our Christmas menu:

What did we serve first? _____

_____

For the main course we had _____

_____

For dessert we had _____

_____

After dinner we had _____

_____

_____

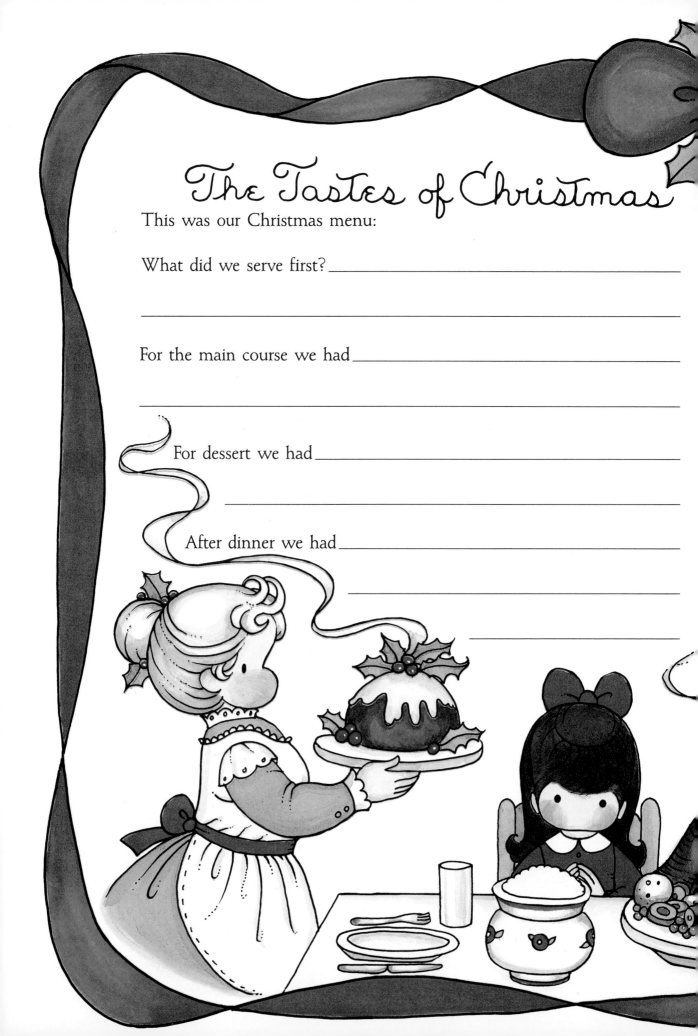

During the Christmas season, my family always has special treats:

Special cakes we like: _____

_____

Christmas cookies we like: _____

_____

Christmas candies we like: _____

_____

Other special dishes: _____

_____

My favorite Christmas food:

Draw a picture.

Write the recipe.

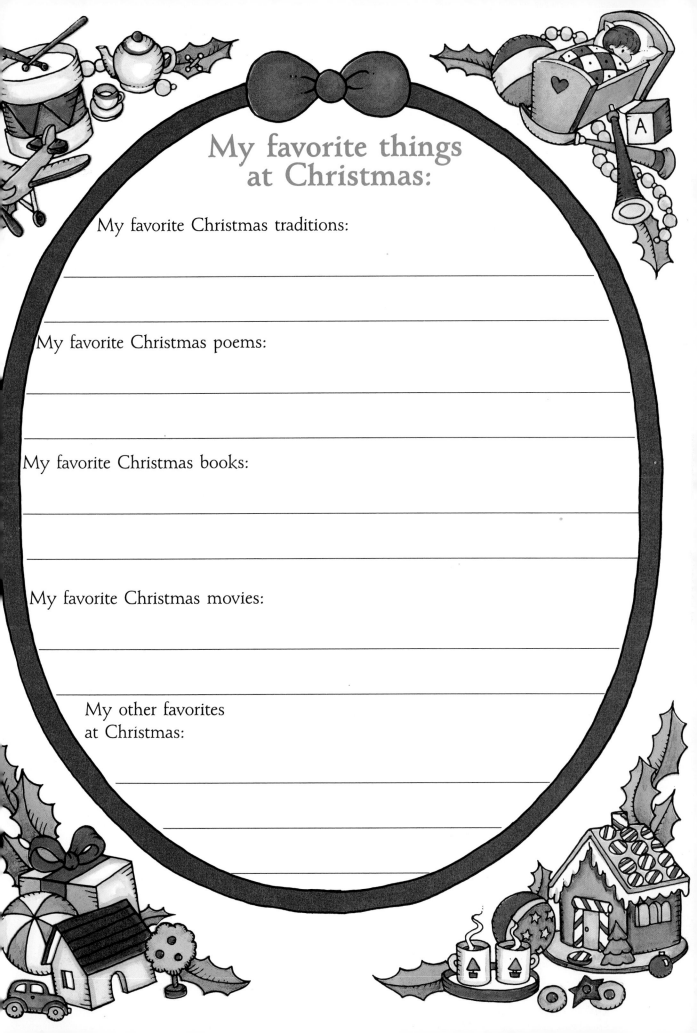

My favorite things at Christmas:

My favorite Christmas traditions:

_____

_____

My favorite Christmas poems:

_____

_____

My favorite Christmas books:

_____

_____

My favorite Christmas movies:

_____

_____

My other favorites
at Christmas:

_____

_____

The Symbols of Christmas

Santa Claus

The name comes from St. Nicholas, a fourth-century bishop who, on hearing of three poor girls, secretly dropped three bags of gold in their window. When they woke up, they found the gift they needed so.

After his death he was made a saint, and the legend of the secret giver of gifts spread throughout the world and continues to this day.

Candy Canes

represent the crooks of the shepherds who came to worship the newborn Baby Jesus on Christmas Eve.

The Bells

The joyous ringing of Christmas bells has been heard from church steeples at Christmastime throughout the centuries. Bells proclaim the happy news of the birth of Jesus in Bethlehem.

The Christmas Stocking

In Europe many years ago, the fireplace was the only source of heat, so the children hung their stockings to dry by the fire. When Santa Claus came down the chimney the first thing he saw was the children's stockings...so that's where he hid his tiny gifts for them.

Candles in the Window

Placing candles in the window began in the Middle East, the birthplace of Jesus, where the flame would light the Christ child's way on his journey.

The Crèche

is the French word for *cradle* or *crib*. St. Francis of Assisi made the first crèche for the people in his parish to help them celebrate the nativity.

Poinsettia

The red poinsettia is the best known floral symbol of the season. In 1828, Dr. Joel Poinsett, America's first foreign minister to Mexico, sent cuttings of the flowering plant as gifts to his friends back in the United States.

Holly and Mistletoe

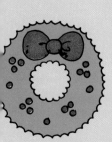

The green of the holly and mistletoe represents the symbol of life through the long, cold winter. The ancient Romans celebrated the rebirth of new life during the festival of Saturnalia by decorating their homes with green wreaths and garlands.

The Yule Log

"Yule" comes from the Scandinavian *Juul.* After the shortest day of the year, the Norsemen would burn a large log in honor of Balder, the God of Light, to celebrate the end of winter.

My Christmas Eve

Christmas Eve is the
magic moment of Peace on Earth,
when all the hurry and busy-ness
finally ends — and the joy and wonder begin!

On Christmas Eve, in my family, we always:

Hang stockings ☐   Sing carols ☐   Go to church ☐

Have a special dinner ☐   Visit friends ☐

Have a family celebration ☐   Wrap presents ☐

Put presents under the tree ☐   Open presents ☐

Travel back home ☐   Sit by the fire ☐   Tell stories ☐

Leave cookies and milk for Santa ☐

Lie in bed wishing ☐   Fall asleep listening for reindeer ☐

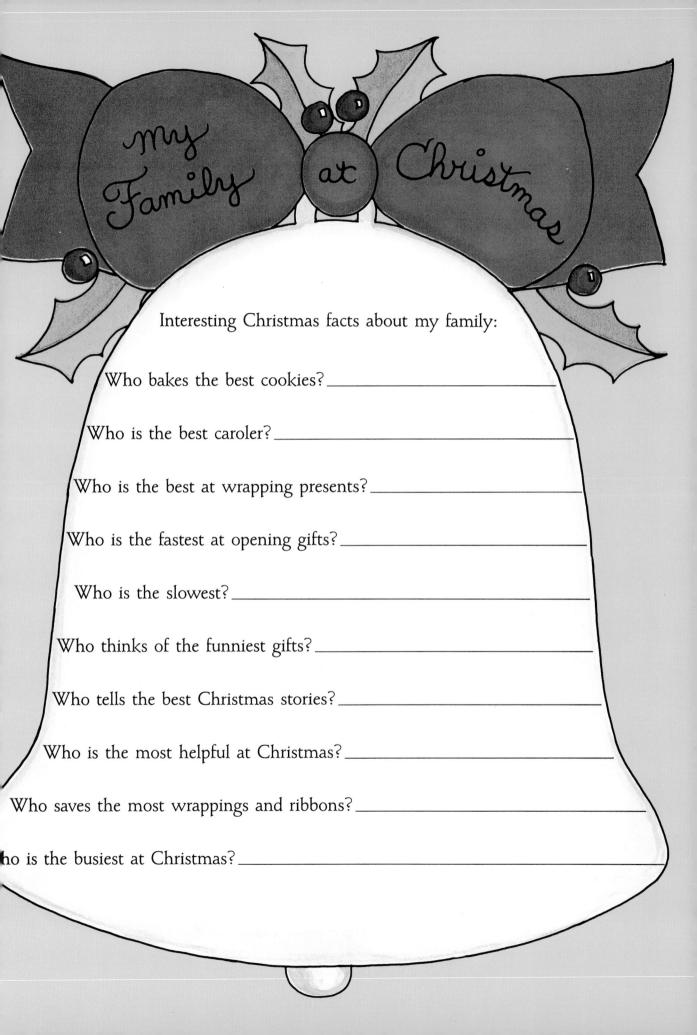

My Family at Christmas

Interesting Christmas facts about my family:

Who bakes the best cookies? _____

Who is the best caroler? _____

Who is the best at wrapping presents? _____

Who is the fastest at opening gifts? _____

Who is the slowest? _____

Who thinks of the funniest gifts? _____

Who tells the best Christmas stories? _____

Who is the most helpful at Christmas? _____

Who saves the most wrappings and ribbons? _____

Who is the busiest at Christmas? _____

My
Christmas
Day

December 25, _____
(year)

Write down the story of your Christmas Day.

A Quilt of my Favorite Christmas papers

Cut out pieces of your favorite wrapping paper and paste in place to make a Christmas Remembrance Quilt.

My Christmas Night

In the evening we _____

_____ and _____.

Who was there? _____

_____

At _____ it was time to go to _____.
o'clock

First, I said my _____, then

I turned out the _____, and before I

closed my _____, I thought to myself,

"This was a Christmas I will always remember!"

Merry Christmas to
all...and to all
A GOOD NIGHT!

My Memories of Christmas

(paste photo)

This is me at Christmas

(paste photos)

These are my friends and family

(paste photo)

This is our Christmas tree

Christmas is Love from Family and Friends who are Far Away!

Sometimes we can't be with the ones we love at Christmas...but even though we are miles apart, in our thoughts and in our hearts we can still be close.

Who always remembers to call at Christmas?

_____

_____

Who writes a special letter? _____

_____

Who sends pictures? _____

_____

Who sends tapes? _____

_____

Whom do you miss *especially*? _____

_____

My Special Christmas

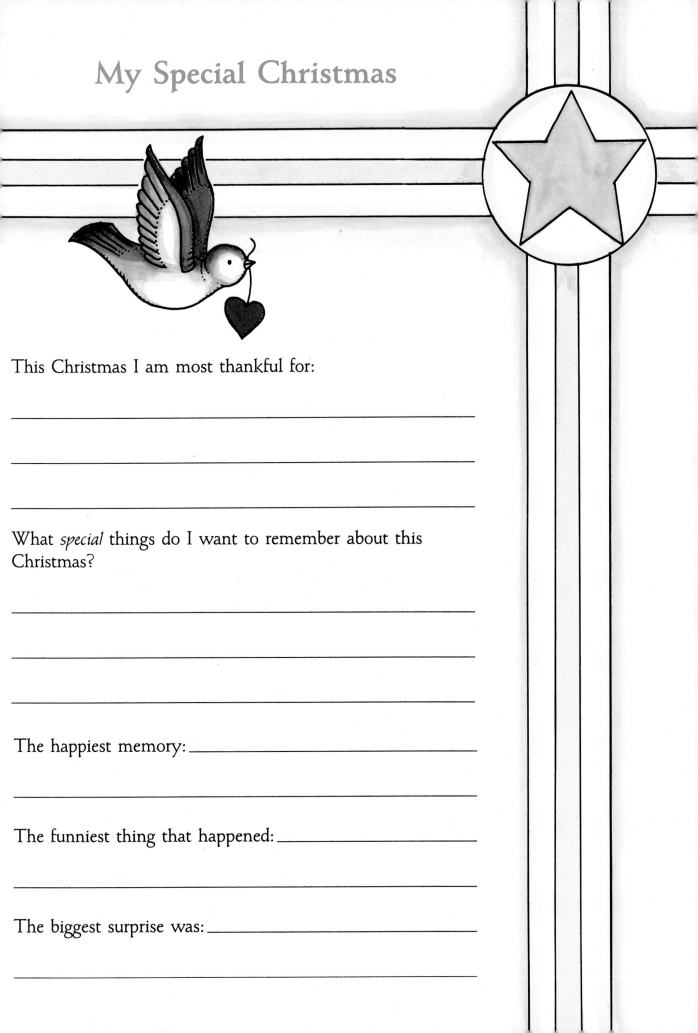

This Christmas I am most thankful for:

_____

_____

_____

What *special* things do I want to remember about this Christmas?

_____

_____

_____

The happiest memory: _____

_____

The funniest thing that happened: _____

_____

The biggest surprise was: _____

_____

My Christmas

Autographs

Now Christmas Day is over
and it's time for me to sleep
But first I'll give a prayer of thanks
for the memories I'll keep.

... the caroling, the candy canes
... the Christmas tree so tall,
... the stockings, and the presents
... the holly in the hall.

I won't forget the laughter
... the wondrous joyful scenes
... and, most of all,
... the Love we shared,

... for that's what Christmas
means!